Reflection of Her
Poems of Memory and Grief

By Rachel Norman
R&R Publishing

Reflection of Her: Poems of Memory and Grief
© 2025 Rachel Norman

This is a work of creative nonfiction. Names, characters, and incidents are drawn from the author's personal experiences and imagination. Any resemblance to actual persons, living or dead, is purely coincidental unless otherwise stated.

Published by:
Randrnorman Publishing LLC
, Flat Rock, MI

ISBN: 979-8-218-17838-3
Library of Congress Control Number: [Optional, if you obtain one]

Cover Design: Rachel Norman
Book Design: Randrnorman Publishing LLC

Printed in the United States of America

Dedication Page

I dedicate this book to my mother and to all the motherless daughters walking this journey. Losing a mother changes you in ways words can never fully capture. It leaves a space, a silence, a longing that time cannot completely heal.

Yet in that emptiness, reflections of her remain—shining in the way we love, the way we stand, the way we carry on. Hold tightly to those reflections. Let them live in you, shaping the woman you are and becoming the echoes of your story.

Table of Contents

Notes:-- 60

Notes:-- 61

Notes:-- 62

Notes:-- 63

Notes:-- 64

Notes:-- 65

Notes:-- 66

Notes:-- 67

Notes:-- 68

Notes:-- 69

Notes:-- 70

Notes:-- 71

Notes:-- 72

Notes:-- 73

Notes:-- 74

Notes:-- 75

Notes:-- 76

Notes:-- 77

Notes:-- 78

Notes:-- 79

Notes:-- 80

Notes:-- 81

Notes:-- 82

Notes: --83

Notes: --84

Notes: --85

Notes: --86

Notes: --87

Notes: --88

Notes: --89

Notes: --90

Notes: --91

Notes: --92

Notes: --93

Notes: --94

Notes: --95

Notes: --96

Notes: --97

Notes: --98

Notes: --99

Notes: --100

Foreword

Grief is a language we never choose to learn, yet it shapes us in ways we could never imagine. Losing a mother leaves an absence that no words can truly fill. And yet, through poetry, reflection, and memory, pieces of that love can be gathered and carried forward.

In *Reflections of Her,* Rachel Norman has taken the raw ache of loss and transformed it into something both deeply personal and universally human. These poems are not only about her mother but about every mother whose love lingers in the lives of her children, even after she is gone. They remind us that while grief carves a hollow space, love continues to echo, shaping us long after goodbye.

This book is more than a tribute; it is a hand extended to every motherless daughter, every grieving heart, every soul who has looked in the mirror and seen traces of someone they miss. Within these pages, sorrow and beauty coexist. There is pain, but there is also resilience. There is longing, but also the quiet reminder that love does not die—it reflects, it echoes, it lives on in us.

As you read these words, may you find not only Rachel's story but pieces of your own. May her reflections stir your memories, comfort your grief, and remind you of the unbreakable bonds we share with those we have lost

Preface

This book began with grief. When my mother passed, I felt as though the ground beneath me shifted forever. The poems in *Reflections of Her* were born out of that space — moments when I needed to give voice to the silence, to name the ache, and to remind myself that love never truly leaves.

For a long time, these words were just for me — a way to survive the empty chair at holidays, the milestones missed, the echoes of her voice that lingered in my memory. But as the years passed, I realized that grief is not just a private burden. It is something we share, something that connects us to one another. Every daughter who has lost a mother, every child who has carried an absence, knows this ache.

So, I offer these poems not only as a reflection of her, but as an invitation. They are an invitation to remember, to mourn, to hope, and to honor. They are reminders that while grief changes us, it also softens us, deepens us, and calls us back to the love that shaped us.

Writing this collection has been both a wound and a healing. I hope that as you turn these pages, you will find your own reflections — of the ones you've loved and lost — and be reminded that though their stories ended too soon, their love lives on in you.

— *Rachel Norman*

Acknowledgment

This book could not have come into being without the love, encouragement, and faith of so many.

First, I thank God, who has carried me through seasons of grief and given me words when I felt I had none. Without His strength, I would not be able to turn loss into healing or pain into purpose.

To my family — thank you for walking this road beside me, even when it wasn't easy. To my children, who remind me every day that love continues, and legacies live on, you are my joy and my reason for pressing forward.

To my friends who listened, encouraged, and reminded me that sharing these poems mattered — your support has been a light in the darkest places.

To every motherless daughter and grieving heart who will hold these pages in their hands — this is for you. I pray these words help you feel less alone and remind you that love leaves echoes that time cannot erase.

Finally, to my mother, this book is yours as much as it is mine. Your reflection lives on in me, and in every word I write.

Introduction

Reflection of Her is more than a book of poems—it is a mirror of memory, love, loss, and the enduring presence of my mother.

When she passed, my world cracked open. I found myself clinging to the fragments she left behind: a smile in my own reflection, a lesson stitched into my bones, a warmth that lingered even in her absence. Grief has a way of echoing through the years, reshaping birthdays, holidays, and the simplest of days into reminders of *what should have been*.

These poems are my attempt to gather those echoes and give them shape. They are whispers of conversations I wish I could still have, prayers I lift when the silence is too heavy, and memories that refuse to fade even as time moves forward.

This collection is not only for my mother, but for every daughter, son, sister, brother, or friend who has ever lost someone too soon. It is for anyone who has looked in the mirror and caught a glimpse of the one they've lost living on within them.

Her story did not end with her passing—it continues in me, and in every reflection of her love that remains. These poems are pieces of that story, offered as both a remembrance and a reminder: that love does not die.

Part One
Reflection of Her

Faded Reflections

Her face drifts further every year,
like whispers I can barely hear.
The edges blur, the colors fade,
A fragile ghost my mind has made.

Her hands once held the weight of mine.
Now only shadows intertwine.
Her voice, a song I can't replay,
it slips like mist at the break of day.

I reach for her in dreams at night,
but morning steals the fleeting sight.
Only fragments now remain,
A tender ache, a gentle pain.

Though time may dim the lines I knew,
the love she gave still shines through me.
A faded memory, soft, unclear,
yet in my soul—she lingers near.

Her reflection

I see her in the quiet glass,
A softened gaze, a shadow passed.
Her laughter lingers in my smile;
her patience carries me each mile.

The way she brushed the morning light
now rests within my hands tonight.
Her voice, though gone, still speaks in me,
A hymn of love, an endless sea.

I trace the echoes in my face,
the tender strength, the gentle grace.
Her heartbeat carved the path I tread,
Her whispers guide the words I've said.

Though time has passed, love remains;
it weaves through loss, through joy, through pain.
I am the mirror, clear and true,
her reflection shining through.

Forever Empty Chair

At every feast, at every prayer,
There waits a forever-empty chair.
Its silence speaks, its shadow tells,
Of broken ties and hollow wells.

Each holiday, each fleeting day,
Your absence stains the light that stays.
The laughter dims, the joy feels thin,
Haunted by what "should have been."

The children know you through my voice,
Through borrowed tales, they have no choice.
They'll never see what parts you are,
The hidden sparks, the subtle hue.

Your stories lost, your wisdom gone,
Yet in our hearts you still live on.
A ghost that lingers in the air,
Beside that forever-empty chair.

Preserving Her

I press her name between the pages,
Whisper stories through the ages,
Trace her face in photographs,
Hold the echoes, fractured halves.

I stitch her voice into my song,
Repeat her words to keep them strong.
I cook her meals, I wear her rings,
To bind her soul to living things.

The world forgets, but I will keep,
Her laughter folded where I sleep.
Though time may steal and shadows blur,
My heart will always shelter her.

I am the keeper, she the flame,
Each breath I take repeats her name.
Though death has claimed what life once gave,
Her memory I vow to save.

Motherless Motherhood

I cradle new life in weary hands,
yet reach for yours, no longer stands.
The gentle guide, the knowing tone,
I'm a mother now, but not alone.

For in each lullaby I weave,
Your voice is there, though I still grieve.
In every touch, in every tear,
I search for you, I feel you near.

But birthdays pass you never see,
The milestones you once dreamed for me.
Advice unsaid, the stories gone,
The thread of you I carry on.

I am a mother, shaped by loss,
A bridge of love, no matter the cost.
Though time erased the life we knew,
I raise my child with parts of you.

Reflections of Her

I see her in the morning light,
A whisper soft, yet burning bright.
The way I move, the way I stand,
Is shaped by her unseen hand.

Her courage lingers in my chest,
Her gentleness in how I rest.
In every smile, in every tear,
The truth remains—she's always nearby.

Though time has stolen her embrace,
Her spirit dwells within my face.
The mirror shows not only me,
But all she dreamed that I could be.

Her love is carved in every line,
A legacy that still is mine.
And though the world may call her gone,
Reflections of her carry on.

The Woman I Became

The years have slipped like falling rain,
Soft and steady, laced with pain.
Seasons turned, yet none could show,
The path I walked you'll never know.

I learned to stand without your hand,
To carve my place, to make my stand.
But oh, how often I would trade,
The strength I built for love you gave.

Each birthday candle burned in vain,
A quiet wish you'd come again.
Through laughter shared and tears I hide,
I feel you walking by my side.

The mirror holds a face so new,
Yet still reflects the parts of you.
Though you were gone, I still became,
A woman shaped by loss—and flame.

And in my bones, in all I do,
The woman I became holds you.

Her Reflection in Me

I catch her glance in mirrored glass,
A fleeting echo from the past.
The curve of cheek, the tilt of chin,
Reminds me where my roots begin.

Her laughter hums beneath my own,
Her patience planted seeds long grown.
The way I move, the words I say,
Are pieces of her, still at play.

She walks within my every stride,
Though years have placed her on the other side.
A quiet strength, a tender grace,
Still lingers softly in my face.

Though death has drawn the lines apart,
Her rhythm beats within my heart.
And even gone, she'll always be,
Alive reflected back through me.

Five Years Gone, A Child Born

Five years had passed since you were near,
When cries of new life filled the air
A tiny hand, a fragile start,
And still the ache within my heart.

You never held the child I bore,
Nor kissed his cheeks, nor loved him more.
The stories lost, the wisdom too,
I tell him now they came from you.

Your absence marked those tender days,
A shadow cast in quiet ways.
I wished you were there to see him grow,
To teach him things I'll never know.

Five years you'd gone, yet love remained,
Through joy and loss, through hope and pain.
And in his eyes, I sometimes see,
A glimpse of you still lives in me.

Not Supposed to Be This Way

It wasn't supposed to be this way,
Your chair still warm, your laugh at play.
But time rewrote what love had planned,
And life moved forward, hand in hand.

I see him now, he smiles again,
A gentleness returned to him.
Her presence soothes the ache he bore,
She gives him peace, she gives him more.

Still, part of me resists the truth,
It feels like treason to our youth.
As if your place could be replaced,
As if his love for you erased.

Yet when I watch, I understand,
This wasn't theft, but life's demand.
She holds him well, she helps him heal,
And in her care, his joy is real.

It wasn't meant to be this way,
But love found light beyond the gray.
Though grief remains, I've come to see,
Her kindness, too, is gift to me.

The Courthouse Vows

No aisle of flowers, no bridal song,
It felt too hollow, felt all wrong.
For how could I, in lace and light,
Stand without you that sacred night?

So, in a courthouse, plain and small,
I signed my name, I gave my all.
No rows of chairs, no dancing floor,
Just quiet vows behind the door.

The papers stamped, the rings exchanged,
A life begun, yet rearranged.
For in that moment, bittersweet,
Your absence echoed at my feet.

I told myself it hurt too much,
To dream of veils, your guiding touch.
So simpler vows would have to do,
A marriage made without you too.

But even here, where joy was bare,
I felt your spirit in the air.
And though no wedding bells were true,
My every vow was tied to you.

Her Granddaughter's Birth

A cry arose, so pure, so new,
A tiny life, the sky turned blue.
Her fingers curled, her heartbeat strong,
A piece of us to carry on.

And oh, I wished that you could see,
This child who bears our history.
Her eyes, her smile, a trace, a spark,
Of you still glowing in the dark.

The cradle rocks where love now grows,
A legacy she'll never know.
I'll tell her stories, sing her name,
So she will feel you just the same.

Though you were gone before her day,
Your spirit shines in her sweet way.
For in her laughter, clear and true,
I see the best of me—and you.

Her Story, My Steps

I swore I'd never walk her way,
I'd carve new roads, I'd choose, I'd stay.
But years have turned, and now I see,
Her story winding into me.

The same soft sighs, the weary hands,
The battles fought, the shifting sands.
Her echoes haunt the life I build,
Her silent wishes unfulfilled.

I catch myself in words she said,
A ghostly script, a thread of red.
The choices mine, yet strangely hers,
The past reborn, the present blurs.

And though it stings, I understand,
The strength she gave was not unplanned.
Through mirrored steps, through loss and flame,
Her history shapes the one I became.

Eleven Years Later

Eleven years had marked the day,
Since she was carried far away.
Her laughter gone, her voice turned still,
Yet love remained, it always will.

And then the news—another blow,
Her brother's light now dimmed and low.
A piece of her was lost again,
A chapter closed where it began.

He held her stories, kept them near,
The ties of blood, the bonds so clear.
Through him, her presence lingered on,
Until the day he too was gone.

Now two are missing from our thread,
Two voices silenced, two lives shed.
Yet in their absence, shadows weave,
A legacy we still believe.

For though the years may steal away,
Their spirits walk each day.
And in our hearts, they both remain,
Together whole, beyond the pain.

Cap and Gown

They said I wouldn't, said I couldn't,
That dreams like mine don't last.
But I kept walking, slow and steady,
Past every shadow of the past.

The nights were long, the tests were heavy,
I stumbled, but I did not fall.
For every voice that told me *"never,"*
I learned to rise above it all.

And now I stand, the tassel turning,
The cap and gown upon my frame.
A woman forged through doubt and fire,
With pride that none can take or claim.

I see her smile—my mother's memory,
I feel her warmth within the crowd.
I've carried her through every struggle,
And now I make her spirit proud.

This moment isn't just my victory,
It's proof of strength they couldn't see.
They said I wouldn't, but I did—
And now the world will answer me.

Seventeen Years Later

Seventeen years since you were gone,
I carried your memory, tried to be strong.
I whispered your name through every storm,
A motherless child in a world reformed.

And then, the cruelest twist of fate,
Another loss at sorrow's gate.
Your daughter taken, oldest, dear,
The wound reopened, sharp and clear.

Two empty chairs now haunt my days,
Two voices missing in life's praise.
I hear you both in fleeting dreams,
Then wake to silence, split at the seams.

I reach for her as I once for you,
The grief is old, the grief is new.
A double shadow walks with me,
Across the years, eternity.

Seventeen years, the circle spun,
A mother lost, now lost a one.
And though I ache, I feel you near,
Two loves I'll carry—forever here.

The Ripple

Her absence fell into my life
Like a stone into still water—
The rings spread wide, unending,
Reaching places I never thought they'd go.

It wasn't just the silence at the table,
Or the empty chair on holidays.
It was the quiet lessons that vanished,
The recipes left untaught,
The wisdom I had to learn alone.

I taught myself how to stand in heels,
How to braid hair, how to soothe pain.
I stitched together pieces of her memory
To build the woman I needed to become.

But even now, the water still trembles.
Every milestone, every change,
Echoes with the waves she left behind.

Her loss was not a single moment—
It was a lifetime altered,
A ripple that will never end.

And yet, in the reflection of that water,
I see her face,
Guiding me still,
Even through the breaking.

Two Absences

I lost her to the silence of the grave,
The final goodbye I could not save.
Her voice a shadow, her touch a dream,
Gone too soon, like a fading stream.

And though my father's heart still beats,
His footsteps echo in distant streets.
Alive, yet gone, too far away,
Another absence I face each day.

So, I built my world with empty hands,
Taught myself what life demands.
No mother's guide, no father's call,
I learned alone to stand at all.

The dresses sewn, the tears I dried,
The lessons missed, the years denied.
Two different losses, yet both the same,
A hollow echo I cannot name.

And still I rise, though bruised, undone,
Carrying the weight of two as one.
For even through the ache I bear,
Their love still lingers, everywhere.

The Distance He Chose

When she was gone, the world grew thin,
And grief drew walls I couldn't climb in.
Her brother, blood, a tether near,
Faded away, too drowned in fear.

It hurt too much for him to stay,
So silence carved the only way.
No visits came, no letters wrote,
Just absence wearing sorrow's coat.

I longed for ties to keep her close,
For stories told, for what he knows.
But distance grew, a heavy wall,
Another loss inside it all.

And still I wonder, still I grieve,
For what was lost, for what could be.
His silence is a second death,
Another ghost that grief bequeaths.

Yet even so, I keep the flame,
Her love is strong, it speaks her name.
Though distance broke what should have been,
She lives in me, she lives within.

The Days You Missed

The candles burn, the children cheer,
But still I ache—you're not here.
Each birthday wish, each frosted cake,
Reminds me of the loss I take.

Their laughter fills the autumn air,
On holidays when love should share.
Yet in the room, a shadow stays,
The empty space of all your days.

They grow so fast, they never knew,
The touch of arms that once were you.
They only know through tales I tell,
Of how you loved us all so well.

But every milestone, every year,
I whisper soft, *I wish you were here.*
The moments gone, the memories missed,
A life reshaped by grief's cruel fist.

And though you never saw them play,
Your love still marks their steps each day.
For in their joy, in all they do,
A piece of you is shining through.

Breaking the Curses

Caps tossed high into the sky,
another chain left far behind.
Grandkids walking, heads held tall,
Defying the whispers that doubted us all.

We came from pain, from storms, from scars,
But still they have reached beyond the bars.
The family curses tried to bind,
Yet they could not defeat the mind.

Each diploma, each proud cheer,
Rewrites the story, year by year.
From broken roots, a garden blooms,
From ashes rise these brighter rooms.

They are the proof, they are the flame,
That cycles end, that hope can reign.
Grandkids crossing that sacred stage,
Turning sorrow into a brand-new page.

And though she's gone, I know she sees,
Her legacy in victories.
For every curse now fades away,
As they step boldly into day.

Reflection of My Mother

When I look within the glass,
Her shadow rises, soft, steadfast.
The curve of cheek, the steady eyes,
A legacy that never dies.

Her voice now lingers in my own,
Her lessons carved me, stone by stone.
The way I love, the way I give,
Are echoes of the life she lived.

Though years have pulled her far away,
Her spirit breathes through me each day.
I find her strength when I am weak,
I hear her wisdom when I speak.

The woman I am, the woman I'll be,
Carries her always, endlessly.
For even gone, she stays in view—
My mother's reflection, shining through.

Speak No Ill

She's gone beyond your words of stone,
She rests where love has made its home.
Your whispers fall on hollow ground,
But cannot shake what I have found.

For every slight, for every sneer,
I hold her memory fierce and clear.
Your shadows cannot dim her light,
Her truth still burns, unbroken, bright.

It says more of you than it of her,
That bitterness is all you stir.
For I have seen the love she gave,
The countless hearts she tried to save.

So, speak your venom, let it fly—
It dies before it meets the sky.
Her legacy is mine to keep,
A mother's love runs vast and deep.

And when I stand, I stand as proof,
Her goodness lives beyond your truth.
No tongue can mar, no lie erase,
The love she left, the life, the grace.

Their Lies Could Not Unmake Her

They twisted words, they bent her name,
Spoke shadows clothed in borrowed shame.
Their stories dripped with bitter hue,
But none of them were ever true.

For I had seen the life she gave,
The gentle hands, the heart so brave.
They spun their lies, but still I know,
The seeds she planted, how they grow.

It speaks of them, not her, at last,
To slander love now in the past.
For when she breathed her final day,
She took no venom on her way.

Their tongues can't stain, their whispers fall,
Her light still shines, it outshines all.
The truth I hold, the love I keep,
Is buried deep where lies can't reach.

So let them talk, let rumors stir,
I'll never doubt the soul she was.
For I'm the proof, her living song—
And truth has silenced lies so long.

Reflection of My Mother

In the mirror, I catch her face,
A fleeting glance, a tender trace.
The curve of smile, the steady eyes,
Her spirit lives, it never dies.

Her laughter lingers in my own,
Her strength is carved into my bones.
The way I stand, the words I say,
Are echoes of her, day by day.

Though time has taken her from view,
Her love remains, both fierce and true.
She shines in me, in all I do,
A reflection clear, a living proof.

For though she walks the earth no more,
Her heartbeat hums within my core.
The mirror shows what I can't see—
She still lives on, reflected in me.

What Should Have Been

Her life was more than sorrow's thread,
A gentle soul the world misread.
She carried dreams no one could see,
Of all she was, of what could be.

She should have had a brighter song,
A thousand years where she belonged.
Her laughter rising through the years,
Not silenced early, drowned in tears.

She should have seen the grandkids play,
Their birthdays, candles, holidays.
She should have danced at weddings near,
Her voice a blessing we could hear.

Instead, the story turned too soon,
Her sun went down before its noon.
And what remains is love, and pain,
And questions asked again, again.

Yet in my heart, her light still glows,
A strength she gave, the love she chose.
Her life cut short, her story thin—
But I still dream what should have been.

Mother Without a mother

I rock my child in midnight's hush,
her breath a rhythm, soft and slow.
But in the silence I feel the crush—
the weight of love I long to know.

I braid her hair with trembling hands,
the way you once would braid mine too.
I give her all my heart commands,
but ache for all I lost with you.

Who do I call when doubt takes hold?
Who steadies me when storms appear?
The world feels heavy, vast, and cold
without your voice to guide me here.

I mother on through grief and strain,
a seed still growing in the dark.
Each tear I shed, each hidden pain,
still feeds the fire, still lights the spark.

For though you're gone, I see your face
in every smile my daughter shows.
Your love lives on, it leaves a trace—
a legacy the heart still knows.

So, I will mother, worn, yet true,
with broken pieces stitched by grace.
Each time she laughs, I'm mothered too—
through her, I find your warm embrace.

Too Young, Too Soon

Her story closed before its prime,
A life unfinished, stolen by time.
Pages torn from the book of years,
Left us clinging to love—and tears.

Too young to leave, too much undone,
Her race had only just begun.
Dreams unspoken, plans unmade,
A future lost in grief's cascade.

She should have had more nights, more days,
To see her children find their way.
To laugh at dawn, to dance at noon,
Not slip away—too young, too soon.

And still her flame refuses dark,
It lingers softly, leaves a mark.
Though time was cruel and life unfair,
Her spirit breathes in every prayer.

Gone too early, yet love remains,
A pulse that runs through all my veins.
Her story ended, but I know—
Through me, her chapters still will grow.

A Letter to My Sister

Dear Sister,

If words could cross the veil of time,
I'd write you lines in gentle rhyme.
I'd tell you still, though I am gone,
My love for you keeps holding on.

We shared our secrets, laughter, tears,
A bond unbroken through the years.
And though my story closed too fast,
The thread we wove will always last.

Please dry your eyes, don't carry blame,
Remember me in joy, not shame.
For though my body rests in clay,
My spirit walks with you each day.

Hold closes the children, teach them well,
The stories only you can tell.
Through you my name will still remain,
A song of love that conquers pain.

So, when the nights feel long and cold,
Think of my arms, your hand I hold.
Dear Sister, know this truth is true:
A piece of me still lives in you.

With love beyond the reach of years,
—Your Sister

To My Love

My love, my life, my dearest friend,
Our story met a sudden end.
I never planned to leave so soon,
To fade beneath a grieving moon.

I see the weight you try to bear,
The empty nights, the vacant chair.
I wish my hands could hold you still,
To calm the storm, to bend your will.

But know this truth, though time divides,
I walk with you on unseen tides.
Your laughter blooms, I linger near,
Your sorrow falls—I feel each tear.

And if you find another's care,
Please take her love, for I am there.
Not as a ghost to chain you down,
But as a blessing, soft, profound.

Remember me in gentler days,
In quiet prayers, in morning rays.
My heart is yours, forever true—
Even in death, I live with you.

Motherless Advice

How do I mother without her hand?
How do I learn, how do I stand?
Her wisdom gone, yet in my chest,
I hear her voice: *just do your best.*

What She Missed

She missed the laughter, missed the tears,
Missed birthdays stacked like falling years.
The grandkids' smiles she'll never see,
Yet still they carry her in me.

Unanswered Questions

Who do I ask when life feels cold?
Who guides me now as I grow old?
Her silence teaches, strange but true,
To trust myself the way she'd do.

Daughter's Ache

A daughter's ache is hard to name,
Both love and loss, both joy and pain.
For every step I take ahead,
I walk with her, though she is dead.

Breaking Chains

The curses fell, but love remained.
I broke the chains my mother chained.
Her strength in me, her fire in kind,
I free the past, I free my mind.

Reflections Eternal

Her eyes are mine, her smile the same,
Her light still shines, it speaks her name.
Though death has drawn its cruel line,
Her reflection lives in this life of mine.

If I Could Have Held You

My daughter, I saw the storms you faced,
The cruel words hurled, the tender erased.
The bruises hidden, the silence deep,
The nights you cried yourself to sleep.

I wasn't there to guard your name,
To shield your heart from all that shame.
But if my arms could break the chain,
You'd never have endured such pain.

Please know, my love, it wasn't you,
The wrongs they gave were never true.
Their violence carved, their voices tore,
But none could change the soul I bore.

You are not broken, you are not less,
You rose from shadows, nonetheless.
And every scar upon your skin,
I hold with love, not marked by sin.

If heaven grants me just one prayer,
It's whispering healing through your air.
That you may stand, unbowed, complete,
A woman whole, a heart that beats.

So, when you doubt, look up, you'll see—
My strength, my love, still lives in thee

To My Strong One

My child, I watched you bear the weight,
Of battles far too harsh, too great.
While others faltered, broke, or ran,
You stood unshaken, took a stand.

Your shoulders carried more than most,
Yet still you loved, you gave, you chose.
You wore your strength like second skin,
Though I know the storm that raged within.

You learned too young to guard, to fight,
To be the pillar through the night.
And though the world may call it pride,
I see the tears you learned to hide.

But strength is more than steel or stone,
It's gentleness that's all your own.
It's rising up when hope feels small,
It's choosing love in spite of all.

So, when you doubt, remember this—
Your strength was born from what I miss.
You are my echo, tried and true,
The strong one—yes—but soft one too.

And if I could, I'd take that weight,
So you'd have space to simply wait.
But since I can't, I'll say it clear:
I am so proud you're still here.

What I Want You to Know

My child, if I could speak once more,
I'd leave you words worth keeping sore.
Not warnings, not regrets, not pain—
But truths to hold when storms remain.

I'd tell you this: you are enough,
even when the road is rough.
You don't have to earn my pride;
it's stitched in you, it will abide.

I'd want you strong, but soft as well,
To know it's safe when tears may swell.
That broken hearts can still grow new,
and healing hands are found in you.

I'd want you never to forget,
The past may hurt, but don't regret.
For every scar has made you whole,
Each mark a chapter of your soul.

And most of all—I'd say with love,
I watch you still from high above.
When life feels heavy, when shadows grow,
remember this: *I love you so*

39

To My Grandchildren

My darlings, though I'm far away,
I watch you grow with every day.
I never held your tiny hands or walked with you in shifting
sands.

But in your laughter, soft and true,
A piece of me still shines in you.
Your mother's love, your family's care,
are proof my spirit lingers there.

Be kind, be brave, and stand up tall,
let love be louder than the fall.
Dream without fear, live without shame,
for life is more than wealth or name.

When birthdays come, when candles glow,
remember this: I love you so.
And though we never met in time,
you'll always, always still be mine.

What I Want You to Know

Mom, if heaven grants you sight,
I hope you see I've lived the fight.
The broken days, the nights I cried,
But still I stood, I still survived.

I want you to know, I've carried you near,
In every step, in every year.
Your strength became the core of me,
The roots that held my dignity.

I've raised my children with your name,
Told them your stories, kept your flame.
So even though they never knew,
they've grown with love that came from you.

I want you to know, I've stumbled too,
but each time I fell, I thought of you.
And in my heart, I heard you say,
Keep walking, child, you'll find your way.

I want you to know, I miss you still,
an emptiness I can't quite fill.
But more than pain, more than sorrow's glow,
I want you to know—I love you so.

Together in Heaven

I dream of heaven's golden shore,
Where tears can't fall, where pain's no more.
And there I see, so pure, so true,
A mother's arms embracing you.

My sister runs, her face alight,
Into the warmth of heaven's sight.
She finds the love she lost too soon,
Restored beneath God's endless noon.

And by her side, a child so dear,
My sweet niece smiles, her spirit clear.
They laugh together, hand in hand,
A family whole, in promised land.

Though earth feels heavy, dark with loss,
I lift my eyes to heaven's cross.
For one day I will join them there,
No broken hearts, no empty chairs.

Until that day, I hold them near,
Their love still whispers, soft, sincere.
A mother, sister, niece all free,
Alive in God's eternity.

Her Mother's Arms

When heaven opened wide its door,
She stepped inside, afraid no more.
The pain was gone, the night was done,
Her journey ended, her race was won.

And there she saw, through light so true,
The one she'd missed, she always knew.
Her mother's face, her mother's smile,
Her mother's arms stretched wide the while.

No need for words, no time to speak,
Just tears of joy on both their cheeks.
The years apart all washed away,
Eternity began that day.

I picture them in heaven's glow,
The love I lost, the love they know.
And though I ache, I find release,
They've found each other, they've found their peace.

Her Sister's Tears

Her sister grieves a double way,
For what was lost, for what can't stay.
Together bound, together torn,
She weeps for her, I weep for more

The Years Between

Each year a brick, each year a wall,
Her voice grows faint, yet I recall.
The years between us stretch so wide,
But love still flows from the other side.

Becoming Her

I used to fight the mirror's truth,
Her shadow in my tender youth.
I swore I'd never walk her way,
I turned from her in fear each day.

But time has hands that shape the soul,
It carves us into something whole.
And as I grew, I came to see,
Her love was planted deep in me.

The way I laugh, the way I cry,
The fire that won't let dreams just die.
The stubborn will, the gentle care,
The strength to stand when none were there.

I tried so hard to not be her,
But life revealed what I prefer:
I'll wear her courage, bear her name,
And honor all from where I came.

For now, I know, I'm proud to be,
The parts of her that live in me.

Her Sister, Her Nieces

Her sister wept, a bond undone,
Two lives once braided into one.
The laughter shared, the secrets kept,
Now silence lingers where she wept.

And nieces, too, were pulled away,
Bright sparks of life that could not stay.
The threads unraveled, one by one,
A tapestry come half-undone.

For grief is cruel—it steals, it breaks,
It leaves behind a trail of aches.
A family tree with branches bare,
So many missing, not all there.

Yet still we hold the names in prayer,
The love that loss could not impair.
Though time may take and shadows fall,
Their memory weaves through it all.

Her sister's tears, her nieces' song,
Remind me where my roots belong.
Though death has claimed what we adore,
Their love still echoes evermore.

With Lisa Again

Through heaven's gate she softly came,
No more sorrow, no more pain.
The angels sang, the light was clear and waiting there was Lisa
dear.

Two smiles met, two arms entwined,
the years of loss left far behind.
Their laughter rose, so pure, so free,
A song of love, eternity.

They shared the stories left unsaid,
the tears we wept, the prayers we pled.
And in that place, where hearts don't break,
they found the joy no time can take.

Though I remain on earth to grieve,
this vision helps my soul believe:
They walk together, hand in hand,
At peace, at home, in the promised land.

Twenty-Eight Years

Twenty-eight years have come and gone,
yet still your shadow lingers on.
The seasons turned, the children grew,
but every year still circles you.

September's wind still chills my bones,
A date that's carved, a truth well-known.
The world moved forward, time marched fast,
but part of me stays in the past.

Twenty-eight candles never lit,
Twenty-eight stories left unfit.
The laughter lost, the love delayed,
the empty chair where memories fade.

And yet, though decades steal their due,
my heart still beats because of you.
For grief may age, but love won't die,
It lifts me still, it keeps me nigh.

So, on that day, I'll pause, I'll pray,
and honor you in my own way.
Twenty-eight years, yet still I see,
You live through love you left in me.

Thank You

Thank you for taking the time to read *Reflection of Her*. This book is one of the most personal pieces of my heart — a way of honoring my mother and the love she left behind. If these poems touched you, reminded you of your own mother, or helped you feel less alone in your grief, then this collection has done what I hoped it would.

If you connected with these words, I invite you to also read my companion book, *Echoes of Me: Poems of Loss and Healing*. Together, these collections tell a story of both memory and rediscovery — the love we hold onto and the self we learn to find again.

I am deeply grateful for every reader who joins me on this journey of memory, healing, and love.

Stay connected with me for more poetry and reflections:
▌ Instagram: **@author_RachelNorman**

TikTok @authorrachelnorman
⊕ Website: **randrnorman.com**

Your support means the world — and if this book spoke to you, please consider leaving a review to help others find it too.

Other Books by Rachel Norman

Reflection of Her

A tender collection of poems written in memory of my mother — her love, her presence, and the ways she shaped my life. These poems are the reflections of her legacy, the mirror of who she was to me, and the light she left behind.

Echoes of Me

Where Reflection of Her ends, Echoes of Me begins. This collection carries the weight of my grief and the steps I took to walk through my mother's passing. It is the sound of my healing, the echoes of my voice learning to rise again, and the poetry of survival and faith.

Together, these two books form a conversation: one looks back at the beauty of her life, while the other reveals the journey of moving forward after loss.

I Surrender, God (Yearly Prayer Journal)

A journal created for those who are ready to lay their worries and battles at the feet of God. With space for prayers, surrender, and reflection, this book is a guide to finding peace through letting go and trusting Him daily.

Thankful, Grateful, and Blessed (Yearly Prayer Journal)

A gentle reminder to see God's blessings in every season. This yearly journal is filled with space to record gratitude, prayers, and reflections — helping you stay rooted in thankfulness, no matter what life brings.

"These works are pieces of my heart — my grief, my healing, and my faith poured onto the page. May they meet you in your own story and remind you that even in loss, love and hope remain.

About the Author

Rachel Norman is a writer, poet, and storyteller whose work is rooted in faith, resilience, and the enduring power of memory. Through her words, she captures the rawness of grief, the beauty of healing, and the strength found in carrying forward the legacies of those we love.

Reflections of Her and *Echoes of Me* were born from Rachel's own journey of losing her mother and learning to navigate life, love, and motherhood without her. Her poetry reflects both the ache of absence and the hope found in remembrance, offering comfort to others who walk the path of loss.

When she's not writing, Rachel is deeply passionate about faith, family, and creating safe spaces where stories of pain can be transformed into testimonies of strength. She hopes her words will remind every reader that though loss changes us forever, love has the power to echo through generations.

A Space for Your Healing

Loss has a way of shaking us to our very core. It can feel heavy, lonely, and unexplainable. In those moments, words may be the last thing we think we have — yet writing can become a powerful tool for healing. Putting your heart on paper is a way of letting your pain breathe, giving your thoughts a safe place to rest, and slowly untangling the knots grief leaves behind.

I encourage you to always pick up the pen. Write your story, your feelings, your prayers, your poems, or even a single word that captures your day. Let your words carry the weight you don't have to hold alone. Sometimes the act of writing is not about creating something perfect — it's about creating a space to heal.

The next few pages are for you. Fill them with whatever you need: notes, poems, lyrics, prayers, or even just raw scribbles of emotion. This space belongs to you, and it is here to remind you that your voice matters, and your healing matters.

And please, remember you don't have to walk this journey alone. If your grief feels too heavy, if you ever find yourself thinking of harming yourself, there is help.

📞 **National Suicide Prevention Lifeline: 988**
(Available 24/7, free and confidential)

Your story is not over. Keep writing, keep breathing, keep holding on.

Notes:

Write something you miss about your mom.

Notes:

Write about a memory you will always cherish.

Notes:

Write about a moment where she made you feel special.

Notes:

Forgive yourself for any pain you caused. Write about
how that looks.

Notes:

Write something you wish you could tell your mother.

Notes:

Write about anything.

Notes:

Write about a special feature of your mom.

Notes:

Write about your earliest memory of your mother.

Notes:

Describe a moment when your mother made you laugh until your stomach hurt.

Notes:

What was her favorite song, scent, or flower?

How does it make you feel now?

Notes:

Write down a holiday or tradition that reminds you of her.

Notes:

What is the greatest lesson your mother taught you?

Notes:

Write about a time when her advice guided you in a difficult decision.

Notes:

What value did she pass on to you that you carry today?

Notes:

Write about a skill you learned from her.

(Cooking, gardening, sewing, working hard, etc.)

Notes:

If you could speak to your mother today,

what would you want to tell her?

Notes:

Write a letter to your mother today
telling her what you miss.

Notes:

How has grief changed the way you see life?

Notes:

How has your view of Mother's Day changed?

Notes:

Write about the ways you've grown stronger,

because of her absences.

Notes:

How do you keep her memory alive, and

How do you pass on her memory to your kids?

Notes:

Create a list of traditions or rituals you want to carry on in her honor.

Notes:

What do you think she would be most proud of you
for?

Notes:

What physical objects of hers do you treasure, and why?

Notes:

If you could sit with your mom today, what is the first thing you would tell her?

Notes:

What qualities of your mother do you see in yourself?

Notes:

How has losing your mom shaped who you are today?

Notes:

Free Write

Notes:

If your grief were a color, what would it look like today? Why?

Notes:

Write a poem about your mom, even if it's just a few lines.

Notes:

How has your relationship with God been impacted by losing her?

Notes:

What do you want others to know or remember about your mom?

Notes:

Imagine your mom writing you a letter from heaven. What would she say?

Notes:

What moments in life do you wish she had been there to see?

Notes:

Write about a way you can honor her memory this week.

Notes:

What emotions are the hardest for you to face in your grief?
Why?

Notes:

How has grief changed the way you love others?

Notes:

Write anything.

Notes:

Free Write

Notes:

Free Write

Notes:

Free Write

Notes:

Write down the parts of your story that feel like they connect you back to her.

Notes:

What does healing look like for you while still holding on to her memory?

Notes:

Write a letter to your mom expressing what you wish you had said.

Notes:

Free Write.